Jings!

WAVERLEY
BOOKS

D1440128

TASTY!

Oor Wullie loves crisps. If you answer the following questions correctly, the letters in the bold box reading downwards will tell you which flavour is his favourite!

1. A very popular pet.
2. A fruit which is the same colour as its name!
3. You use one on your hair.
4. Very busy insect.
5. A drink you can also swim in!
6. Shines at night.

Answers 1. Cat. 2. Orange. 3. Comb. 4. Ant. 5. Water. 6. Moon.

Sweet Treat

Hidden in the wordsquare are sweets which Wullie and his mates love to eat. How quickly can you find them all?

F	L	Y	I	N	G	S	A	U	C	E	R	S
M	U	U	M	A	C	A	R	O	O	N	H	L
D	C	Q	C	Y	D	N	A	C	F	F	U	P
S	K	S	S	K	I	M	P	S	L	U	B	S
P	Y	H	H	S	Y	I	W	U	I	D	A	K
I	T	R	E	N	T	B	M	H	M	G	R	C
L	A	I	R	O	C	P	A	P	P	E	B	A
Y	T	M	B	B	S	G	I	G	S	A	R	J
R	T	P	E	N	N	Y	C	H	E	W	O	K
R	I	S	T	O	F	F	E	E	J	N	C	C
E	E	Y	D	B	M	O	J	O	S	D	K	A
H	S	T	A	B	L	E	T	I	M	P	S	L
C	G	O	B	S	T	O	P	P	E	R	S	B

**BLACKJACKS   BONBONS   CHERRY LIPS
FLUMPS   FLYING SAUCERS   FUDGE
GOBSTOPPERS   IMPS   LUCKY BAG   LUCKY TATTIE
MACAROON   PENNY CHEW   PUFF CANDY
SHERBET DAB   SHRIMPS   MOJOS   TABLET
TOFFEE   RHUBARB ROCK**

One sweet appears five times. Can you find which one?

The sweet which appears five times – Imps

ARITHMETRICKS

Here are a few problems for you to do while I feed Jeemy!

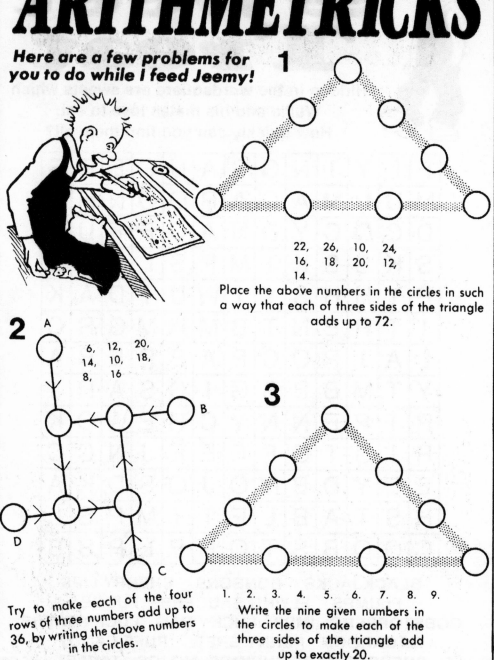

1

22, 26, 10, 24, 16, 18, 20, 12, 14.

Place the above numbers in the circles in such a way that each of three sides of the triangle adds up to 72.

2

A

6, 12, 20, 14, 10, 18, 8, 16

B

D

C

Try to make each of the four rows of three numbers add up to 36, by writing the above numbers in the circles.

3

1. 2. 3. 4. 5. 6. 7. 8. 9.

Write the nine given numbers in the circles to make each of the three sides of the triangle add up to exactly 20.

ANSWERS

1. From the top, reading clockwise – 18, 14, 16, 24, 10, 26, 12, 20, 22.

2. A – 18, 10, 8. B – 20, 6, 10. C – 14, 16, 6. D – 12, 8, 16.

3. From the top, reading clockwise – 5, 3, 4, 8, 1, 9, 2, 6, 7.

FOREST MAZE

WULLIE'S lost in Ben Doon Forest. See if you can guide him through the maze to reach Auchenshoogle.

START HERE

TORN DUNGAREES

See how many words you can make using the letters from " TORN DUNGAREES ".
They must have four or more letters. Plurals and proper names are not allowed.
Each letter should be used only once.

Put your answers in the space below.

HOW DID YOU SCORE?

20 words or less — Try again! 20-40 — Not bad! Over 40 — Jings! See ye on "Who wants to be a Millionaire?"!

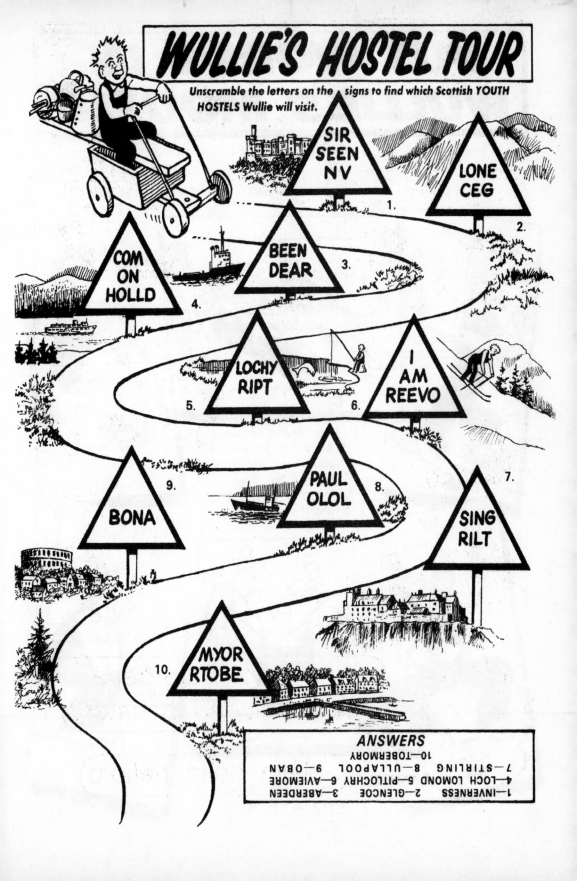

PUT WORDS IN WULLIE'S MOUTH!

That's right! See if YOU can guess what Wullie's saying in each of the pictures below. There are six captions for you to match up with the pictures. Couldn't be easier! Or could it?

1 I hate stewed cabbage!
2 Ma's a braw cook!
3 I ken when I'm licked!
4 I'm in the lolly!
5 He's a smashing pet!
6 MMM! I've waited a' day for this!

ANSWERS

A—6 B—3 C—4
D—5 E—2 F—1

JOIN THE DOTS

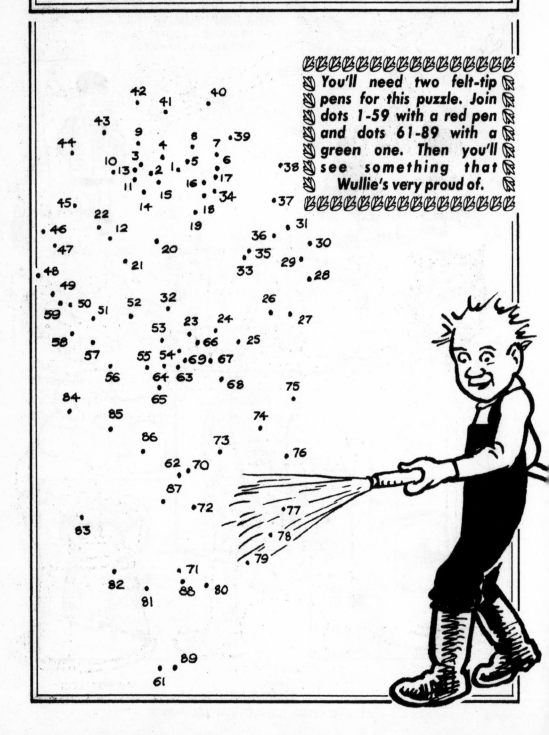

You'll need two felt-tip pens for this puzzle. Join dots 1-59 with a red pen and dots 61-89 with a green one. Then you'll see something that Wullie's very proud of.

WULLIE'S WORKSHOP

I've been busy inventing a few things.
Tak' a look at whit I've made!

BLOW!

Battery-operated
fan spoon for hot soup.

Jigsaw puzzle for Pa.
He's useless at jigsaws.

Book for doing
homework and watch-
ing TV at the same time.

Punch ball for
Jeemy, my pet
mouse.

BEST
POTATOES

Special sack for the
sack race.

My easy chair.

WORD LADDERS

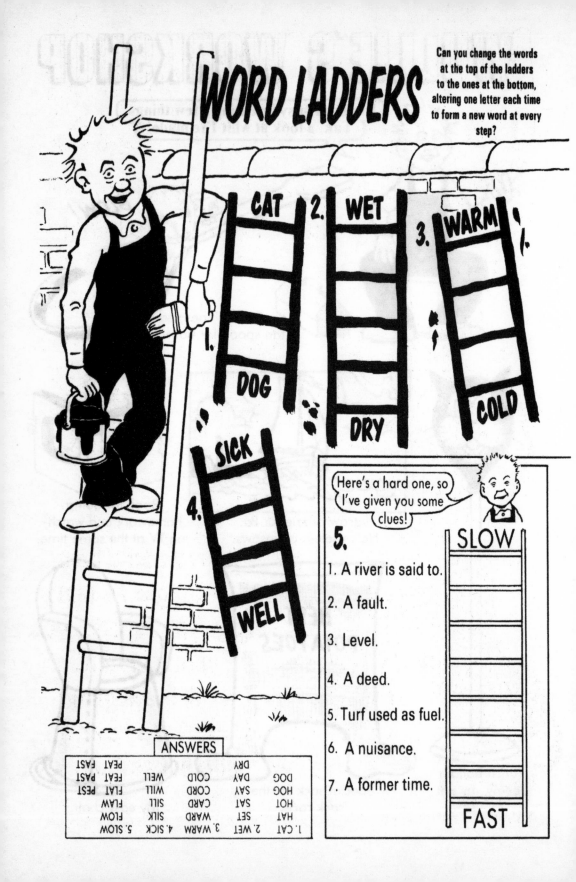

Can you change the words at the top of the ladders to the ones at the bottom, altering one letter each time to form a new word at every step?

1. CAT → DOG

2. WET → DRY

3. WARM → COLD

4. SICK → WELL

Here's a hard one, so I've given you some clues!

5. SLOW → FAST

1. A river is said to.

2. A fault.

3. Level.

4. A deed.

5. Turf used as fuel.

6. A nuisance.

7. A former time.

ANSWERS

1. CAT   2. WET   3. WARM   WILL   WELL   4. SICK   5. SLOW   FLOW   FLAW   FLAT   FEAT   PEAT
HAT   SET   WARD   DOG   SILK   FLAW
SAT   SAY   CARD   CORD   COLD   DAY   SILL   FEAT   PEST
HOT   DRY   DAY   SICK   FAST

Key Words

Answer the following clues to find five words which all have the letters 'key' in them.

1. A hot country and a bird.
2. A jungle animal.
3. You type on one on your computer.
4. A team game.
5. A member of the horse family.

Answers: 1. Turkey — 2. Monkey — 3. Keyboard — 4. Hockey — 5. Donkey

Pocket Money Puzzle

It's Wullie's pocket money day today. Unscramble the letters to discover what he's going to buy!

cei—marec

ptores

iomcc

priscs

hotrc

Answers:
ice-cream, poster, Comic, crisps, torch

JEEMY

Why was the computer in so much pain?

Because it slipped a disk!

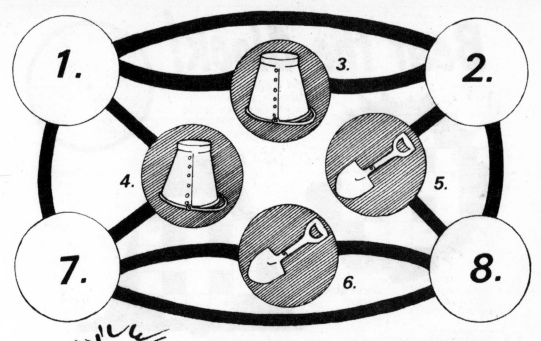

BUCKETS 'N' SPADES

THE OBJECT OF THIS GAME IS TO REVERSE THE POSITIONS OF THE BUCKETS AND SPADES SO THAT THE BUCKETS ARE IN CIRCLES 5 AND 6, AND THE SPADES IN 3 AND 4.

MOVE THEM ALONG THE LINES FROM CIRCLE TO CIRCLE, ONE MOVE AT A TIME, MAKING SURE THAT THERE ARE NEVER TWO IN THE SAME CIRCLE.

USE DIFFERENT COLOURED COUNTERS AS MARKERS FOR EACH MOVE. SEE HOW FEW MOVES YOU CAN DO IT IN.

SOLUTION ➡

1.BUCKET 3 to 2   2.SPADE 5 to 8
3.BUCKET 4 to 1   4.SPADE 6 to 7
5.BUCKET 2 to 5   6.SPADE 7 to 4
7.BUCKET 1 to 7   8.SPADE 8 to 2
9.BUCKET 7 to 6   10.SPADE 2 to 3

Beat the Clock!

HERE ARE SOME SIMPLE CROSSWORDS. USE A WATCH TO SEE WHICH MEMBER OF THE FAMILY CAN DO THEM THE QUICKEST.

1.

CLUES ACROSS
1. CONSUMED
5. DIVIDE AMONG OTHERS
6. A SMALL, INDUSTRIOUS INSECT

CLUES DOWN
2. INSTRUCT
3. INQUIRE
4. AREA OF WATER

2.

CLUES ACROSS
1. A WISE BIRD
5. A MONTH
6. UNUSUAL

CLUES DOWN
2. THE EARTH
3. STOUT
4. NOT NEW

3.

CLUES ACROSS
1. PUSSY
5. CAPTURE
6. FROZEN WATER

CLUES DOWN
2. CAPER
3. PERFORM
4. BASHFUL

4.

CLUES ACROSS
1. A FLYING MAMMAL
3. NATIVE DRUMS
5. QUIVER
6. GIRL'S NAME

CLUES DOWN
1. THESE PROTECT THE FRONT AND BACK OF A CAR.
2. BOTHER
3. SMALL CHILD
4. TO OBSERVE

SOLUTIONS

1.
ACROSS: 1. ATE 2. SHARE 6. ANT
DOWN: 1. TRAIN 3. ASK 4. SEA

2.
ACROSS: 1. OWL 5. APRIL 6. ODD
DOWN: 2. WORLD 3. FAT 4. OLD

3.
ACROSS: 1. CAT 5. CATCH 6. ICE
DOWN: 2. ANTIC 3. ACT 4. SHY

4.
ACROSS: 1. BUMPERS 2. TROUBLE 3. TOT
DOWN: 1. BAT 3. TOM-TOMS 5. TREMBLE 6. SUE 4. SEE

OOR WULLIE'S FUN SECTION

Horace:—"Can you telephone from an aeroplane?"

Pilot:—"Of course I can tell a phone from an aeroplane!"

★★★★★★★★★★★

Customer:—"Are these binoculars powerful?"

Shopkeeper:—"Powerful? Why, when you look through them, ten miles away seems to be behind you."

★★★★★★★★★★★

Gamekeeper—"Don't you know you're not allowed to fish here?"

Sandy—"I'm not fishing. I'm teaching a worm to swim!"

★★★★★★★★★★★

Jack:—"I know a man who shaves twenty times a day!"

John:—"Impossible! Who is he?"

Jack:—"He's a barber!"

Traveller:—"Did you label my luggage for London?"

Porter:—"No, I had to label it for Manchester. We've run out of labels for London!"

★★★★★★★★★★★

Golfer—"I'll stay here until I hit this ball!"

Caddie—"You'll need a new caddie then. I'm going on holiday next week!"

★★★★★★★★★★★

Grandpa:—"I have three pairs of specs. One pair for out of doors and another pair for indoors."

Grandson:—"What is the third pair for?"

Grandpa:—"To look for the other two pairs!"

★★★★★★★★★★★

Bill:—"I spent ten hours on my geography book last night!"

Jim:—"You didn't, did you?"

Bill:—"Yes! I put the book under my mattress and slept on it!"

Mum—"Why don't you start your dinner, Fred?"

Fred—"I'm waiting for the mustard to cool!"

★★★★★★★★★★★

Diner:—"Can I have some game?"

Waiter:—"Certainly, sir. Ludo, or Snakes and Ladders?"

★★★★★★★★★★★

Father:—"Why are you always fighting with the boy next door?"

Jim:—"He's the only boy in the street who's smaller than me!"

★★★★★★★★★★★

Policeman—"Hoi! What's the game?"

Peem—"Football — Rovers versus United."

JIGSAW

No wonder Wullie's running. You would be, too, if you could see what's chasing him. Cut out the pieces to form an animal. Remember to read the jokes over the page before you do this puzzle!

Turn over the next page for the answer.

AH! HERE WE ARE! PAINTED GOALPOSTS! JUST THE JOB FOR SPOT KICK PRACTICE!

JINGS!

ACH, I'M FED UP O' THIS PRACTISIN' LARK! I'M OFF TO THE GAME!

YE'RE THROUGH, WULLIE! SHOOT, MAN!

PENALTY, REF!

YOU TAK' IT, WULLIE!

HERE WE GO!

ACH, NO! I'VE HIT ANITHER POST!

MIND YOU, NOTHIN' DISASTROUS HAPPENED THIS TIME, READERS!

YOU MISSED, YOU STUPID GOWK!

SOME SPOT KICK EXPERT!

JINGS! I'M ON THE SPOT NOW!

C'MERE! WE WANT A WORD WI' YOU!

TIME I WAS AWA'!

ACH! HUMBUG! I'VE BEEN POSTED TO THE RESERVES — POST HASTE!

What do you call a bird on rollerblades?

A cheep skate!

ANSWER TO 'JIGSAW' PUZZLE

True or false

Wullie's fed up because heis got extra homework to do. Can you help him answer the questions? Answer true or false.

1. A pistachio is a type of nut.
2. A prairie dog is actually a rodent.
3. A tambourine is a wind instrument.
4. A group of tigers is called a pride.
5. One of the Seven Dwarfs was called Woody.
6. A tamarin is a type of monkey.
7. Paris is the capital of France.
8. A male swan is called a pen.
9. Greyfriars Bobby was a dog.
10. Spaghetti comes from Greece.

Answers: 1. True. 2. True. 3. False — you beat it. 4. False — it's a streak. 5. False. 6. True. 7. True. 8. False — it's a cob. 9. True. 10. False — it comes from Italy.

DR. WULLIE'S CASEBOOK

Wee Eck's been fighting again, and Dr. Wullie's been called out to give him treatment. However, the artist has already given Eck "treatment". Only two pictures of Eck are exactly alike. Can you spot them?

ANSWER

C and H are the same.

GUESS WHAT?

What do these strange drawings represent?
Can you help Detective Wullie solve the mysteries?

ANSWERS

1. WALKING STICK, 2. DORMOUSE, 3. BREAKFAST,
4. MAN WITH SPOTTED BOW-TIE CAUGHT IN SLIDING
DOORS, 5. LONG BOAT, 6. HIGH TEA, 7. WATCHDOG,
8. FISH SUPPER, 9. CAR BOOT, 10. BOWLER HAT,
11. CHEESE ROLL, 12. SPRING ONION, 13. BUTTERFLY.

TREE TEASERS

A

1. LOOK! THERE'S A BEE, CHRISTINE!

2. I FOUND A WASP IN EVERY APPLE.

3. THAT WASN'T FUNNY, EWAN.

4. WE HAVEN'T A MAP. LET'S BUY ONE.

5. THE PALACE HAD MANY BEAUTIFUL ARCHES.

THE NAME OF A TREE IS HIDDEN IN EACH SENTENCE. CAN YOU FIND THEM?

B

1. ØPKIØNE
2. LGAIRFCH
3. ABILRPCHM
4. ALPIMREE
5. GPUULMM
6. LSPRUMCEE
7. PPLEEAACMH

EACH GROUP OF LETTERS CONTAINS THE NAMES OF TWO TREES. CAN YOU CROSS OUT THE LETTERS OF ONE TREE IN EACH GROUP TO LEAVE THE NAME OF ANOTHER READING ACROSS? WE'VE CROSSED OUT OAK TO LEAVE PINE TO GIVE YOU A START.

C

CHEAP

LAPEP

REAP

ABNAAN

REGAON

RE-ARRANGE THE LETTERS IN EACH GROUP TO FIND THE NAMES OF FIVE FRUITS.

ANSWERS

C PEACH, PEAR, BANANA, APPLE, ORANGE.

B 2. FIG/LARCH 3. PALM/BIRCH 4. PEAR/LIME 5. PLUM/GUM 6. ELM/SPRUCE 7. MAPLE/PEACH.

A 1. BEECH 2. PINE 3. YEW 4. MAPLE 5. LARCH.

CARTOON TIME

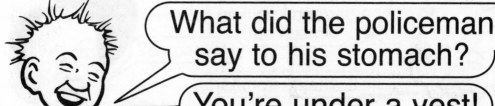

Scottish QUIZ WHIZZ-KID!

It's the only subject Wullie's any good at. See if you are a Scottish Mastermind. (Maybe Mum and Dad can try this one, too!)

NAE BOTHER!

1. A north coast town. You could say its name's a mouthful.
2. A "bright" wee toon in the north-east!
3. Famous, amongst other things, for its magnificent Military Tattoo.
4. A town at the west corner of Loch Tay.
5. The Granite City at the mouths of rivers Don and Dee.
6. This famous canal links Fort William and Inverness.
7. Skye's rocky mountain range.
8. On whose bonnie banks can you watch the "Maid of the Loch"?

9. It's really quite bracing in Angus's "Smokie" town.
10. Name the largest town in the Western Isles.
11. The Queen has often attended Scotland's famous Highland Games. Where?
12. Scotland's city watched over by The Law.
13. A Spanish galleon sank in the bay of which Mull town?
14. What are Argyll's Three Sisters?
15. It's Skye's largest town.
16. Bonnie Prince Charlie cooked Johnnie Cope's goose in this town on the Forth.

17. A world-famous ski resort on the River Spey.
18. RARER ANTS is an anagram of which Scottish port?
19. Scotland's home of golf.
20. "Doon the Watter" from Glasgow, this town's rock isn't for eating.

ANSWERS

1. TONGUE, 2. WICK, 3. EDINBURGH, 4. KILLIN, 5. ABERDEEN, 6. THE CALEDONIAN CANAL, 7. THE CUILLINS, 8. LOCH LOMOND, 9. ARBROATH, 10. STORNOWAY, 11. BRAEMAR, 12. DUNDEE, 13. TOBERMORY, 14. MOUNTAINS IN GLENCOE, 15. PORTREE, 16. PRESTONPANS, 17. AVIEMORE, 18. STRANRAER, 19. ST ANDREWS, 20. DUMBARTON.

WORD SQUARES

Start from certain letters and move to the next letter in any direction to see if you can spell the names of 11 articles of men's clothing. The arrows show how to spell " Tie " to give you a start. You may use the same letters twice in any word.

ANSWERS—

TIE, VEST.
SCARF, SHIRT, SHOES,
GLOVES, HAT, PANTS,
BELT, CAP, COAT,

--- HOW MANY VEGETABLES CAN YOU SPELL? ---

Using the same method as above, now try to find as many vegetables as you can.

ANSWERS —

SPROUT, TOMATO, TURNIP, YAM.
ONION, PARSLEY, POTATO, PEA, SPINACH,
BEAN, CELERY, CHIVE, CRESS, GARLIC, KALE,

Joker in the Pack

WHY IS IT CONFUSING WHEN A DOG GROWLS AND WAGS HIS TAIL AT THE SAME TIME?

YE DINNA KEN WHICH END TAE BELIEVE!

IS IT DANGEROUS TO SWIM ON A FULL STOMACH?

YES – IT'S BETTER TAE SWIM IN WATER!

WHY WAS THE SHEEP ARRESTED ON THE MOTOR-WAY?

COS IT MADE A EWE-TURN!

WHY DOES WEE HARRY CHASIN' A RABBIT RESEMBLE A BALDY-HEIDED MAN?

HE MAKES A LITTLE HAIR GO A LONG WAY!

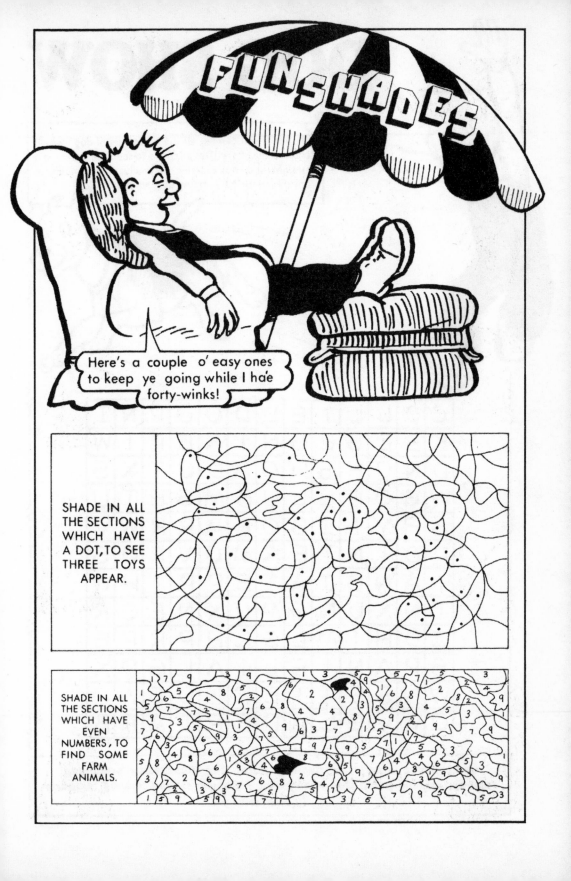

DOG SHOW

See if you can list all the **17** breeds of dog which entered the show. The puzzle is to read the letters in a straight line, horizontally, vertically or diagonally in any direction. (No jumping over squares.)

```
C O L L I E L D O O P N I
K E E S E G N I K E P I W
D N U H S H C A D O T X S
W G O D L L U B M S E T U
S H Y I Z B O E A R R W V
P O I N T E R M O V R O S
I A N B J A T E P P I H W
T N X U N G M U X N E C R
Z D H I M L G L H P R F E
S P A N I E L I A L G D X
W N S E T T E R K D S W O
O W V E L A D E R I A R B
```

ANSWERS:—

Airedale, Beagle, Boxer, Bulldog, Chow, Collie, Dachshund, Pointer, Poodle, Pekingese, Pomeranian, Pug, Setter, Spaniel, Spitz, Terrier and Whippet.

ALL CHANGE!

RATTLE

Can you change the words at the top of the ladders to the ones at the bottom, altering one letter each time to form a new word at every step?

SURE	GOOD	LOSE
1 _____	1 _____	1 _____
2 _____	2 _____	2 _____
3 _____	3 _____	3 _____
4 _____	4 _____	4 _____
5 HAZY	5 BEST	5 FIND

And for you brain boxes, here's one that's a wee bit more difficult! Can you spell three additional animals when you change the word "sow" to "pig" in seven steps? Change one letter to form another word in making each move.

HELP MA BOAB!

SNAP

SOW

1 _____
2 _____
3 _____
4 _____
5 _____
6 _____
7 PIG

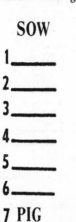

ANSWERS

SOW, COW, how, hoe, DOE, DOG, dig, PIG.

Lose, nose, none, nine, fine, find.

Good, gold, bold, bolt, belt, best.

Sure, pure, pare, hare, haze, hazy.

SEE HOW MANY WORDS OF THREE OR MORE LETTERS YOU CAN MAKE USING THE LETTERS FROM:

'INVERSNECKIE'.

PLURALS AND PROPER NAMES ARE NOT ALLOWED.

PUT YOUR ANSWERS IN THE SPACE BELOW.

INVERSNECKIE

HOW DID YOU SCORE?
20 WORDS – NO' BAD.
30-40 WORDS – PRETTY GOOD.
OVER 40? TOP O' THE CLASS!

OODLES of DOODLES

Can you guess what Wullie's doodles represent?
He's left some of the letters in each of the words,
to help you!

- - U - - - N - R -

H - - R - P - - - -

- - I - G - - S - - P

M - - - B - - -

U - - - L C - - - - - G - - - Y

- - E - - YP - - - -

L - Z - - - - - -

Answers.

Mountaineers, hairyplane, ginger-
snap, moth-ball, jewel-carriageway,
telly-phone, lazy-bones.

OOR WULLIE

A noisy cat? A barking dug?
No, it's Wullie on the loose.
But jings, things really happen when
He imitates a moose!

THAT'S STAN McCROAK, THE ANIMAL IMPRESSIONIST, WULLIE.

HE'S MADE A FORTUNE WI' HIS BIRD SONGS AN' THINGS!

A FORTUNE, EH? I THINK I'LL HAE A GO AT THAT!

I'LL START WI' A CAT MEOWIN'...

MEOW! MEOW!

PESKY CAT! GET OOT O' IT!

CLONK!

JINGS, IT'S DANGEROUS BEIN' A CAT ROOND HERE!

I'LL TRY A DUCK INSTEAD...

QUACK! QUACK!

DR WHA SURGERY

CALL ME A QUACK, EH? HOW DARE YOU?

CRIVVENS!

I'LL HIDE IN THAT KENNEL AN' MAK' A SOUND LIKE A DUG. NAEBODY CAN OBJECT TAE THAT!

BUT...

CHEEK! THERE'S ANOTHER DUG IN MY KENNEL!

BARK!
RUFF!
WOOF!

What room has no walls, floor, ceiling or windows?

A mushroom!

WHAT A BUNCH!

NO WONDER WULLIE'S BLUSHING! HE HAS TO DELIVER THIS BUNCH OF
FLOWERS TO MRS McPHEE. HE DOESN'T WANT TO BUMP INTO ANYONE—OR
ANYTHING! CAN YOU HELP HIM CHOOSE THE SAFEST ROUTE?

FIGURE IT OUT!

2	7	3	5	4	7
6	4	9	6	8	1
8	1	2	4	2	3
5	9	8	3	5	5
9	7	6	1	8	3
4	2	7	6	1	9

Can you divide this large square into four pieces of the same shape and size? Each piece must have nine small boxes containing the numbers 1 to 9 inclusive.

(ANSWER ON NEXT PAGE.)

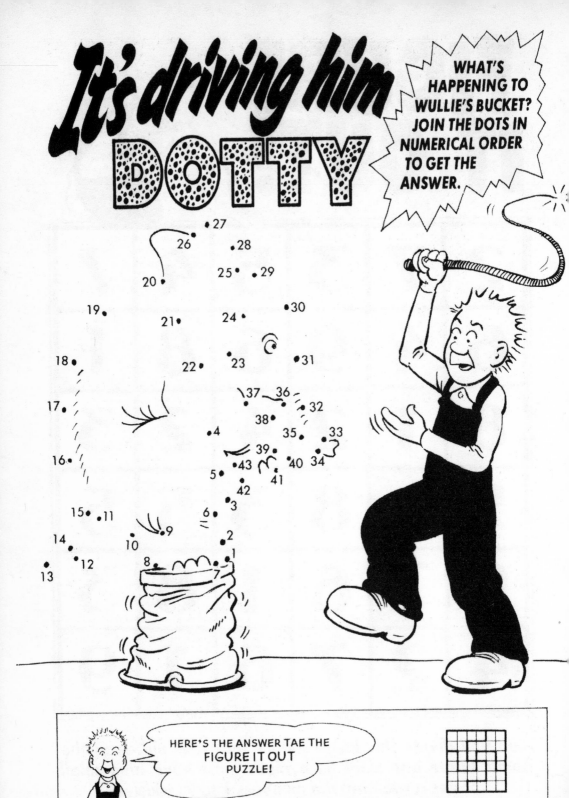

TRICKS TO TRY

It's great how ye can swing a bucket fu' o' water roond yer heid an' yet no' spill a drop. See if yer pals can dae it — then try the other tricks on them!

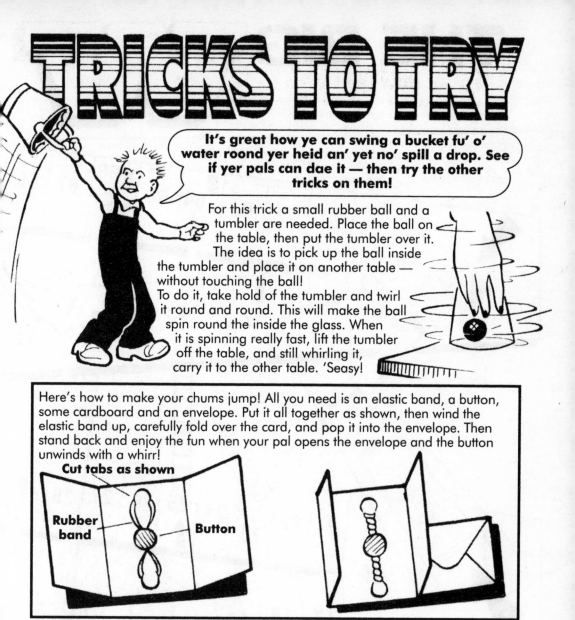

For this trick a small rubber ball and a tumbler are needed. Place the ball on the table, then put the tumbler over it. The idea is to pick up the ball inside the tumbler and place it on another table — without touching the ball!
To do it, take hold of the tumbler and twirl it round and round. This will make the ball spin round the inside the glass. When it is spinning really fast, lift the tumbler off the table, and still whirling it, carry it to the other table. 'Seasy!

Here's how to make your chums jump! All you need is an elastic band, a button, some cardboard and an envelope. Put it all together as shown, then wind the elastic band up, carefully fold over the card, and pop it into the envelope. Then stand back and enjoy the fun when your pal opens the envelope and the button unwinds with a whirr!

Cut tabs as shown

Rubber band **Button**

Here's another tumbler trick! Ask your pals if they can stand a tumbler on a piece of paper which is laid across another tumbler.

Here's how it's done.
Just fold the paper like this and —

HEY PRESTO!

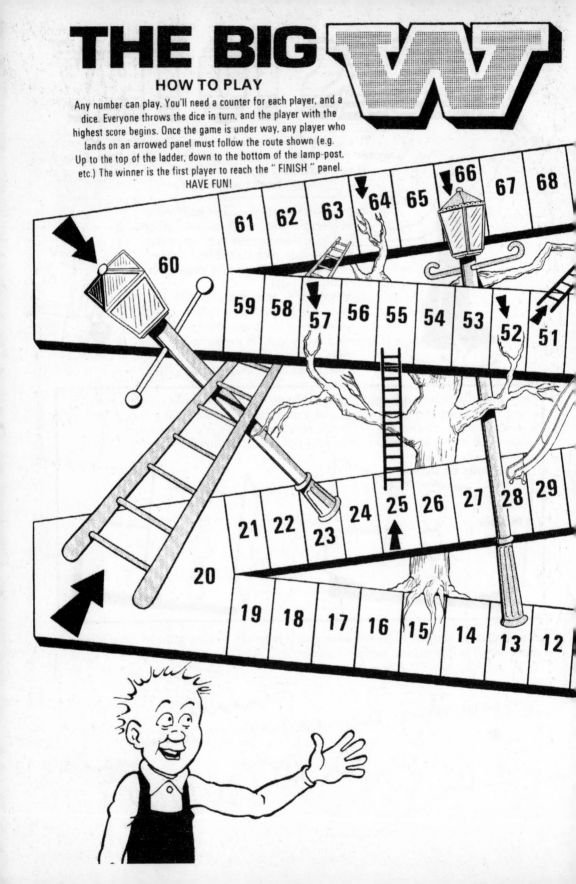

You MUST finish by landing on the " FINISH " panel. If your throw means you will overshoot the panel, then you must wait until your next throw, and until you score the exact number to land on the panel.

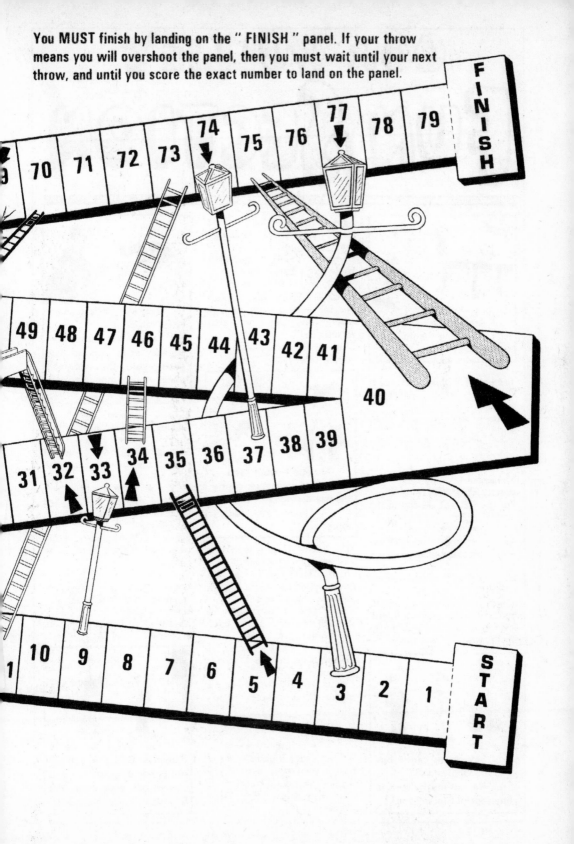

OOR WULLIE'S FUN SECTION

"Are you sure one of us isn't working from the wrong plan?"

Tam—"Will this letter reach Glasgow before tomorrow night?"
Postie—"Aye, it will that, son!"
Tam—"That's funny! It's addressed to Inverness!"

★　★　★

McLaggan—"Why is this station called 'Fish Hook'?"
Porter—"It's at the end of the line!"

★　★　★

Angry Customer—"That watch dog you sold me is no use at all!"
Dog Dealer—"What's wrong with it?"
Angry Customer—"When burglars broke into our house last night, the dog snarled so loudly, we didn't hear them!"

"Say, man, can I buy this zoo for my kids?"
"No, but maybe we can buy your kids for our zoo!"

Fat Fred—"What? Two pounds for a shave? Your sign says one pound!"
Barber—"That's right—but you've got a double chin!"

★　★　★

Gunn—"You just can't imagine what I went through when my car hit that steamroller!"
Lunn—"Oh, yes, I can! The windscreen!"

"I hope I didn't see you looking at your book during the exam, Angus!"
"I hope you didn't either, sir!"

Wee Eck—"How is it that no hair grows on your head?"
Uncle Wull—"What a daft question! Why doesn't grass grow on a busy street?"
Eck—"Oh, it can't get up through the concrete!"

★　★　★

Boarder—"Look, here, I haven't a decent towel, sponge or piece of soap!"
Landlady—"Well you've a tongue in your head, haven't you?"
Boarder—"Yes, but I'm not a cat!"

★　★　★

Bill—"That's a nasty hole you have in your brolly, Bert."
Bert—"Yes, it's there so that I can see when the rain's stopped!"

"I ordered chicken soup. What's this?"
"We didn't have any chicken soup, sir, so we gave you the nearest thing—the water we boil the eggs in!"

Pa—"I wonder why my shaving brush is so stiff?"
Harry—"I don't know! It was all right yesterday when I painted the canary's cage with it!"

★　★　★

First Workman—"Does the foreman know that the trench has fallen in?"
Second Workman—"Well, we're just digging him out to tell him!"

★　★　★

Angus—"All the buses are stopping tomorrow!"
Hector—"Why?"
Angus—"To let the people off, of course!"

"I'm going to be a detective, Dad. Can you tell me a good disguise?"
"Wash your face and nobody will recognise you!"

Word Puzzler

Once you've found the nine-letter word in the boxes, see how many three-letter words you can make from it.

D U N

G A R

E E S

(Clue: you wouldn't catch Wullie in anything else!)

If you scored:
0-5 – Come on, waken up!
6-11 – That's more like it!
12 upwards – Well done!

Note The Difference!

These six pictures of Wullie might all look the same, but if you look closely, you'll see only two are identical. Can you find them?

ˈlɐɔᴉʇuǝpᴉ ǝɹɐ ꓷ puɐ Ɔ

SPOT-ON!

Here's a chance to test your knowledge of Scottish geography. To find the names of each place marked on the map, you just have to solve the given clues!

1. The granite city.   2. The Fair Maid once lived here.
3. McCaig's Folly looks over this seaside town.
4. Robert Burns is buried here.
5. Home of the " theatre in the hills ".
6. Site of the Wallace Monument.
7. Island home of treasure from the Spanish Armada?
8. It's here the only private army in Britain is based.
9. Famed for its bridies!
10. Often referred to as the Highland capital.
11. Affectionately known as " Auld Reekie ".

Answers 1. Aberdeen 2. Perth 3. Oban 4. Dumfries 5. Pitlochry 6. Stirling 7. Tobermory 8. Blair Atholl 9. Forfar 10. Inverness 11. Edinburgh

What starts with a T, ends with a T, has T in it and makes T?

A teapot!

What did one calculator say to the other?

You can count on me!

BE A SPORT!

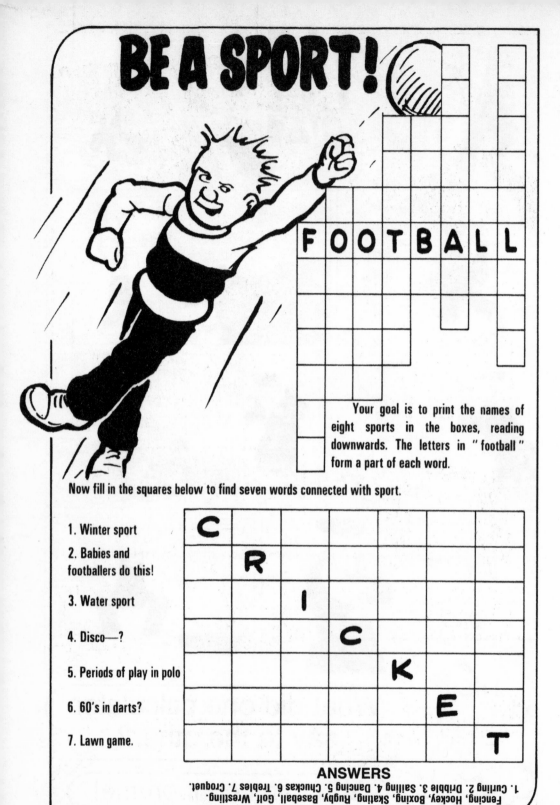

F O O T B A L L

Your goal is to print the names of eight sports in the boxes, reading downwards. The letters in "football" form a part of each word.

Now fill in the squares below to find seven words connected with sport.

1. Winter sport

2. Babies and footballers do this!

3. Water sport

4. Disco—?

5. Periods of play in polo

6. 60's in darts?

7. Lawn game.

C
R
I
C
K
E
T

ANSWERS

1. Curling 2. Dribble 3. Sailing 4. Dancing 5. Chuckas 6. Trebles 7. Croquet.

Fencing, Hockey, Boxing, Skating, Rugby, Baseball, Golf, Wrestling.

RHYME TIME

Oor Wullie's been writing some limericks, but he's left out certain words. Can you fill in the blanks?

THERE WAS A YOUNG MAN NAMED Mc PHEE,
WITH THE FUNNIEST FACE YOU COULD - - - .
AND NOBODY KNOWS
WHERE HE GOT HIS BIG - - - - ,
BUT HE USED IT FOR STIRRING HIS - - - !

SAID THE REF TO HIMSELF, WITH A SIGH,
AS THE WRESTLERS DID HOPELESSLY - - - ,
"IT'S PLAIN THAT THEY'VE GOT
THEMSELVES IN A - - - - ,
SO I'LL HAVE TO DECLARE IT A - - - !"

I WENT A WALK WITH MY FRIEND JIM,
AND SOMEBODY THREW A TOMATO AT - - - .
NOW TOMATOES ARE SOFT,
AND DON'T HURT THE SKIN,
BUT THIS ONE DID, 'COS IT CAME IN A - - - !

BRRRRRRR!

THERE WAS A YOUNG CENTIPEDE NAMED BILLY,
WHO SAID, "I THINK NATURE'S SO - - - - - !
FOR I JUST CAN'T KEEP NEAT
MORE THAN HALF OF MY - - - - ,
AND WHAT CHILBLAINS I GET WHEN IT'S - - - - - !"

Answers: 1. See, nose, tea. 2. Him, tin. 3. Lie, knot, tie. 4. Silly, feet, chilly.

WULLIE'S TOP TEN

HIDDEN IN THESE SQUARES ARE TEN OF WULLIE'S FAVOURITE THINGS OR PEOPLE. THE WORDS ARE WRITTEN ACROSS, UP, DOWN, DIAGONALLY—AND EVEN BACKWARDS! SEE HOW QUICKLY YOU CAN SPOT THEM!

L	L	A	B	T	O	O	F	S
J	P	K	O	J	C	L	E	O
T	C	I	B	P	A	E	Z	A
E	W	Y	T	K	R	F	T	P
K	H	E	M	A	T	J	B	Y
C	G	C	G	E	I	W	K	F
U	R	N	F	N	E	B	X	J
B	U	I	X	Y	M	J	S	R
D	U	M	P	L	I	N	G	P
S	W	Y	T	P	L	B	A	Z

ANSWERS:- FOOTBALL, BUCKET, DUMPLING, DUNGAREES, BOB, ECK, SOAP, JEEM, MINCE, CARTIE.

PUZZLE PLACES

EACH PICTURE REPRESENTS THE NAME OF A PLACE IN SCOTLAND. CAN YOU GUESS ALL EIGHT?

ANSWERS

1. WIGTOWN   2. COATBRIDGE   3. KINGHORN   4. PENICUIK   5. FALKIRK   6. GLASGOW   7. BATHGATE   8. MUSSELBURGH

OOR WULLIE

Fat bob thinks he's smart —
His ploys are really neat.
But Wull strikes back when he becomes
A bobby on the "beat"!

BOYS O BOYS, THAT WIS A SMASHIN' POLICE FILM!

MAJESTIC CINEMA
TODAY
INSPECTOR ASKYEW INVESTIGATES

I'M GOIN' TAE BE A POLICEMAN, TRACKIN' DOON BADDIES!

HIYA, SHORTY!

SHORTY? I'LL PULVERISE YE!

COME OWER AN' TRY IT!

BUT —

LEAP

HO-HO! LOOK, ECK

HE'S IN THE FLYING SQUAD NOW!

PYOINGG!

CLUNK!

AND NOW HE'S IN THE SPECIAL BRANCH!

THAT'S WHIT WE CA' "TREE-MENDOUS" FUN!

I'LL TRACK THAE JOKERS DOON!

HELP!

?

LOOK, BOB — AN UNDERCOVER COP!

What dog smells of onions?

A hot dog!

What's a kangaroo's favourite vegetable?

A spring onion!

EYE · EYE!

ONLY TWO OF THESE BINS ARE EXACTLY ALIKE
CAN YOU HELP P. C. MURDOCH SPOT THEM?

← SILENT

ANSWER Numbers 2 and 9

OOR WULLIE'S CROSSWORD

CLUES ACROSS
3. Long narrow opening (4), 5. Large kind of wasp (6), 7. Snake (5), 8. Delicate (6), 11. Sharp tasting (6), 13. Large sea (5), 14. Set fire to (6), 15. Apple or rhubarb? (4)

CLUES DOWN
1. Close (4), 2. Wading bird (5), 3. Mix up (4), 4. Ripped (4), 6. Late part of the day (7), 9. Undress (5), 10. Worn on the foot (4), 11. Used to catch fish (4), 12. Water grass (4)

SOLUTIONS
ACROSS: 3. Slot 5. Hornet 7. Viper 8. Tender 11. Bitter 13. Ocean 14. Ignite 15. Tart.
DOWN: 1. Shut 2. Crane 3. Stir 4. Torn 6. Evening 9. Strip 10. Boot 11. Bait 12. Reed.

OOR WULLIE

A wee scoot here, a wee scoot there –
This Supa-Foam's just smashin'!
Oor laddie thinks his fortune's made –
But Ma sends his hopes crashin'!

THIS NEW SUPA-FOAM IS MARVELLOUS—IT POLISHES AND CLEANS AT THE SAME TIME.

HMM, I COULD MAK' SOME MONEY WI' THAT!

MA WINNA MIND IF I—ER—BORROW IT!

WID YE LOOK AT THAT LAZY HUSBAND O' MINE, LIZZIE. I CANNA GET HIM TAE CLEAN THE WINDIES FOR ME!

I'LL DAE YER WINDIES FOR YE, MRS BLACK!

GRAND! HERE, TAK' THE BUCKET. I'LL GET YE A CLOTH.

I DINNA NEED WATER. WE WINDIE-CLEANERS USE MODERN METHODS!

WATCH! ONE SQUIRT O' MY WONDER WINDIE CLEANER AN' YER WINDIES WILL BE . . .

AYE, BUT . . .

JINGS, THE WINDIE'S OPEN!

THAT'S WHIT I WIS TRYIN' TAE TELL YE!

YE WEE DE'IL!

THAT'S A RARE HEID O' HAIR YER MAN'S GOT, BELLA!

LATER

DRUMCHUCKIE O.A.P.s CLUB

THIS FLAIR'S TOO STICKY FOR DANCIN', ETHEL!

IT HASNAE BEEN THE SAME SINCE GRANPAW BROON SPILLED SHERBET ON IT!

AYE, AYE, MAIR BUSINESS FOR ME!

A WEE SQUIRT HERE, AN' A WEE SQUIRT THERE, THAT'S THE WAY TAE POLISH YER FLAIR!

Where does a frog keep his money?

In a river bank!

What do ducks like on television?

Duckumentaries!

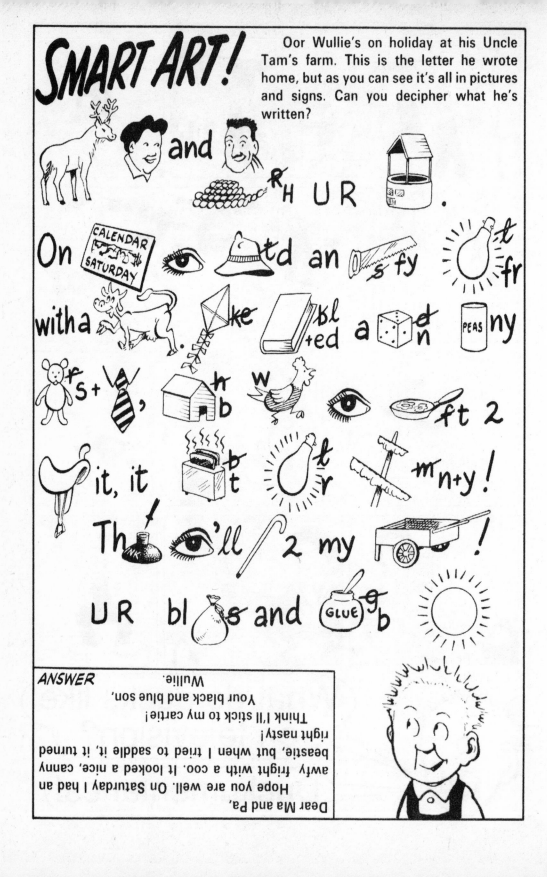

SMART ART!

Oor Wullie's on holiday at his Uncle Tam's farm. This is the letter he wrote home, but as you can see it's all in pictures and signs. Can you decipher what he's written?

ANSWER

Dear Ma and Pa,
Hope you are well. On Saturday I had an awfy fright with a coo. It looked a nice, canny beastie, but when I tried to saddle it, it turned right nasty!
Think I'll stick to my cartie!
Your black and blue son,
Wullie.

QUIZ BIZ!

*Nae wonder Oor Wullie is in the corner!
When teacher asked him who married Mary Queen of
Scots, quick as a flash he answered, "The minister!"
Now see how YOU do in this Scottish quiz . . .*

1. Name the famous Scottish missionary, explorer and doctor who was born in Low Blantyre, Lanarkshire?

2. Where in Kinross-shire was Mary Queen of Scots imprisoned?

3. In which east coast town is the Lammas Fair held?

4. Where would you find the "Soldier's Leap"?

5. Which Scottish scientist changed the whole course of medical treatment by his discovery of penicillin?

6. When was the Tay Road Bridge opened to public traffic?

7. What are "wally dugs"?

8. Which Scottish loch is famed for the reported sightings of a monster?

9. What is the "Roaring Game"?

10. Name the Viking fire festival held in Shetland every January.

11. What is a "spurtle"?

12. Which Greenock-born Scot is credited with inventing the steam engine?

13. When is Burns Night?

14. What is a finnock?

15. What game is played at Rugby Park?

16. Which is farther north, Moscow or Edinburgh?

17. What are the Munros?

18. Name the Scots actor who first played James Bond in the film series.

19. Which Scottish football team is nicknamed the "Red Lichties"?

20. Which famous Scottish athlete was portrayed in the film, "Chariots Of Fire"?

ANSWERS

1. David Livingstone. 2. Loch Leven Castle. 3. St Andrews. 4. Killiecrankie. 5. Sir Alexander Fleming. 6. August 18th, 1966. 7. Ornamental china dogs. 8. Loch Ness. 9. Curling. 10. Up-Helly-Aa. 11. A wooden stick with which porridge is stirred. 12. James Watt. 13. January 25th. 14. A pale or whitish Scottish sea trout. 15. Football. 16. Edinburgh. 17. Scottish mountains over 3000 feet. 18. Sean Connery. 19. Arbroath. 20. Eric Liddell.

CARTIE CAPERS

Try to draw a separate pencil line from each cartie to the place where it is going. You are not permitted to cross or touch another line or touch anything else in the picture, including the border. Draw the lines lightly so they may be easily rubbed out if necessary.

Turn over the next page for the answer.

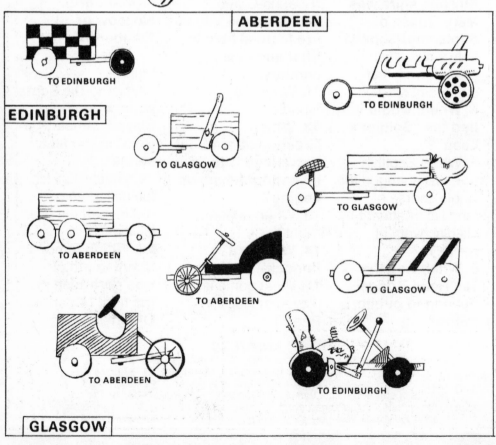

ABERDEEN

TO EDINBURGH

TO EDINBURGH

EDINBURGH

TO GLASGOW

TO GLASGOW

TO ABERDEEN

TO ABERDEEN

TO GLASGOW

TO ABERDEEN

TO EDINBURGH

GLASGOW

SPORTING CHANCE!

In column 'A' is a list of sports and in column 'B' a list of sports personalities.
See how quickly you can match the person to the correct sport.

A TENNIS
RUGBY
GOLF
BOXING
CONKERS
FOOTBALL
SNOOKER
ROWING
CRICKET

B JONAH LOMU
VENUS WILLIAMS
NASSER HUSSAIN
MATTHEW PINSETT
MICHAEL OWEN
TIGER WOODS
LENNOX LEWIS
OOR WULLIE
RONNIE O'SULLIVAN

ANSWERS

TENNIS, VENUS WILLIAMS; RUGBY, JONAH LOMU; GOLF, TIGER WOODS; BOXING, LENNOX LEWIS; CONKERS, OOR WULLIE; FOOTBALL, MICHAEL OWEN; SNOOKER, RONNIE O'SULLIVAN; ROWING, MATTHEW PINSETT; CRICKET, NASSER HUSSAIN.

Cartoon Time

TWO FOR YOU!

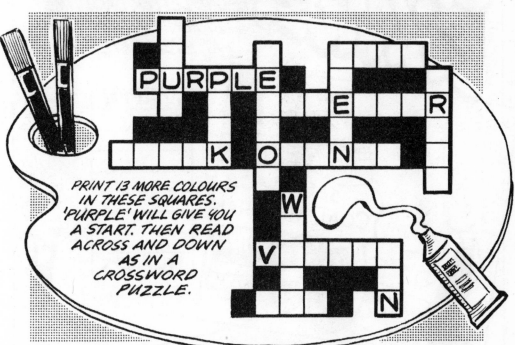

PRINT 13 MORE COLOURS IN THESE SQUARES. 'PURPLE' WILL GIVE YOU A START. THEN READ ACROSS AND DOWN AS IN A CROSSWORD PUZZLE.

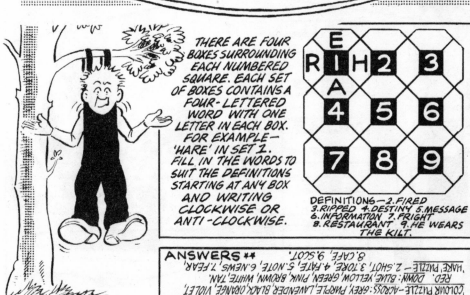

THERE ARE FOUR BOXES SURROUNDING EACH NUMBERED SQUARE. EACH SET OF BOXES CONTAINS A FOUR-LETTERED WORD WITH ONE LETTER IN EACH BOX. FOR EXAMPLE - 'HARE' IN SET 1. FILL IN THE WORDS TO SUIT THE DEFINITIONS STARTING AT ANY BOX AND WRITING CLOCKWISE OR ANTI-CLOCKWISE.

DEFINITIONS— 2. FIRED 3. RIPPED 4. DESTINY 5. MESSAGE 6. INFORMATION 7. FRIGHT 8. RESTAURANT 9. HE WEARS THE KILT.

ANSWERS ✷✷

COLOUR PUZZLE—ACROSS: GREY, PURPLE, LAVENDER, BLACK, ORANGE, VIOLET, RED. DOWN: BLUE, YELLOW, GREEN, PINK, BROWN, WHITE, TAN. 'HARE' PUZZLE — 2. SHOT, 3. TORE, 4. FATE, 5. NOTE, 6. NEWS, 7. FEAR, 8. CAFE, 9. SCOT.

QUICK CHANGE!

CAN YOU CHANGE THE WORDS AT THE TOP OF THE LADDERS TO THE ONES AT THE BOTTOM, ALTERING ONE LETTER EACH TIME TO FORM A NEW WORD AT EVERY STEP?

JAS. BLACK COAL MERCHAN

WHITE

BLACK

SAIL

SHIP

MORE

LESS

JOY

SAD

ANSWERS

WHITE — WHINE, SHINE, SPINE, SPICE, SLICE, SLICK, SLACK — BLACK. SAIL — SAID, SLID, SLIP — SHIP. MORE — LORE, LOSE, LOSS — LESS. JOY — BOY, BAY, BAD — SAD.

HAPPY BIRTHDAY

TODAY IS WULLIE'S BIRTHDAY, AND AS A TREAT, HIS MA HAS LET HIM HAVE HIS FAVOURITE FOOD. AS YOU SEE, HOWEVER, THE LETTERS ARE ALL JUMBLED UP, AND TO DISCOVER WHAT OUR BIRTHDAY BOY IS GOING TO EAT, YOU'LL HAVE TO REARRANGE THE LETTERS.

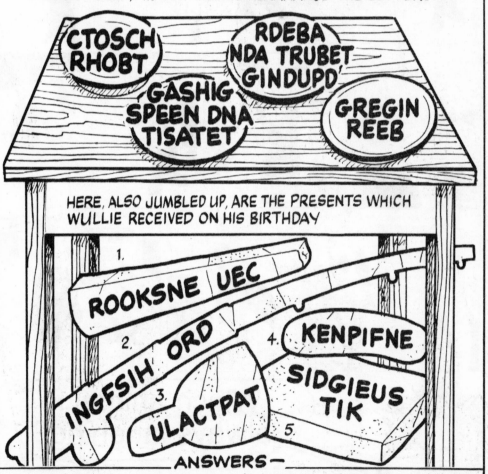

CTOSCH RHOBT

RDEBA NDA TRUBET GINDUPD

GASHIG SPEEN DNA TISATET

GREGIN REEB

HERE, ALSO JUMBLED UP, ARE THE PRESENTS WHICH WULLIE RECEIVED ON HIS BIRTHDAY

1. ROOKSNE UEC

2. INGFSIH ORD

3. ULACTPAT

4. KENPIFNE

SIDGIEUS TIK

5.

— ANSWERS —

FOOD— SCOTCH BROTH, HAGGIS, NEEPS AND TATTIES, BREAD AND BUTTER PUDDING, GINGER BEER.
PRESENTS— 1. SNOOKER CUE, 2. FISHING ROD, 3. CATAPULT, 4. PENKNIFE, 5. DISGUISE KIT.

OOR WULLIE

Wull's headdress looks really tatty,
But he knows what to dot.
Alas, the folks this Injun meets
Go on the warpath too!

IN WULLIE'S SHED

MOTHS

STOOR

DON'T ASK

CRIVVENS, IT'S TIME I GOT SOME NEW FEATHERS FOR MY INJUN HEADDRESS!

I'LL LOOK IN AULD TAM WILSON'S HEN COOP.

BUT...

A'RIGHT—KEEP YER FEATHERS ON!

LATER

JINGS—THERE'S A BIG BURD JUST BEHIND THAT FENCE!

EASY!

SNATCH!

BUT

HELP! MY HAT!

SHRIEK!

SCOUNDREL!

I'LL SNEAK INTAE THE PET SHOP AND SEE WHIT THEY'VE GOT THERE!

RAT SALE

PET SHOP

THIS PARROT WINNA MISS A PUCKLE FEATHERS!

BUT—

HELP!

POLICE!

FIRE!

SSHH!

TRUST ME TAE PICK A BURD THAT COULD TALK!

WEE IMP!

Which animal is always laughing?

A happy-potamus!

A TUNNY FALE

by WOOR ULLIE

WINK

No answers with this one! If you try hard enough, you'll read this tricky tale!

YANY mears ago, when Scatlond was inhabited by wunny fee men kearing wilts and backetty toots, a cad lalled Bandy Sroon came to the Forth of Firth. When he saw that he couldn't seach the other ride without wetting get, he thought he bould wuild a bridge.

He wet to sork with his axe and dopped chown all the mees for triles around. Hoon he sad enough wood to bake a mridge and he spent wany meeks nammering hails fefore he was binished.

At last the dig bay came and trowds cravelled from all carts of the pountry to watch Bandy beclare the dridge open. In his hig bands he held a barge lottle of his granny's mome-hade lemonade which he gas woing to use in the ceremony.

Bandy baised the rottle and announced, "I beclare this dridge trell and wuly open!" Then he bashed the smottle on the bridge.

The pundreds of heople shooked on in lock. Bandy's vork had been in wain. The rottle bemained in one piece but the ridge was in bruins. Piles of wintered splood floated rown the diver.

But it mook tore than this to hiscourage our dero. He made another in only wee threeks but the thame sing happened. Even the third attempt desulted in risaster.

It was not until yundreds of hears later that another midge was brade. Tis thime it was made of stiron and eel and it rarried the cailway from Falmeny to Dife. Because of Bandy's bree thridges they called this one the Fourth Bridge, and that is how we know it to this dery vay.

FUNNY FIZZOGS!

HERE'S A REALLY TRICKY PROBLEM. CAN YOU DRAW JUST TWO STRAIGHT LINES ACROSS THIS OBLONG SO THAT IT WILL BE DIVIDED INTO FOUR PARTS WITH AN EQUAL NUMBER OF OOR WULLIE FACES IN EACH PART?

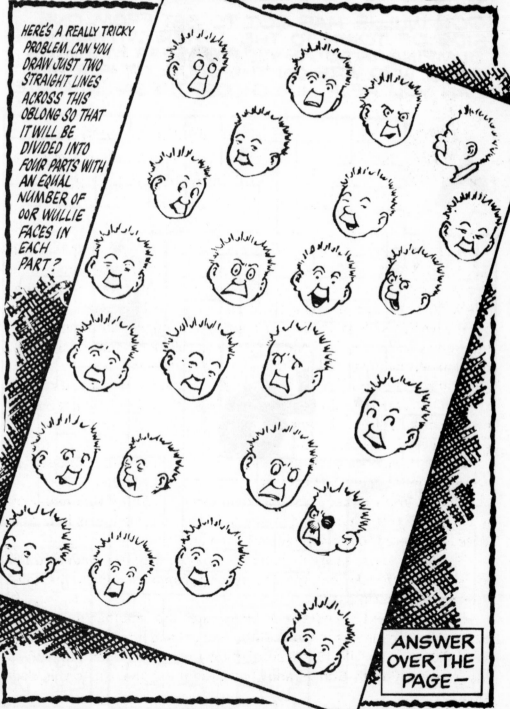

ANSWER OVER THE PAGE—

JUST AMAZING!

OOR WULLIE HAS GOT TO GET FROM ONE SIDE OF TOWN TO THE OTHER WITHOUT BUMPING INTO ANY OF BASHER McTURK'S GANG, WHO ARE ON THE LOOKOUT FOR HIM. CAN YOU HELP HIM CHOOSE THE SAFEST ROUTE?

OOR WULLIE'S FUN SECTION

"Jings, you've got a broken arm! How did it happen?"

"It was through skin trouble—"

"Ye expect me to believe that?"

"Aye, the skin was off a banana!"

Diner—"Waiter! What's this?"
Waiter—"It's bean soup, sir."
Diner—"Never mind what it's been. What is it now?"

★ ★ ★

"What are you doing these days, Gladys?"
"Working on a farm where they raise hornless goats."
"But—"
"There are no butts."

"Am I too late for the collection?"

"Na, na, missus—just climb aboard."

Gent—"I see you are putting up a new house."
Builder—"Well, that's the only kind we put up."

★ ★ ★

Customer (twice nicked by the barber's razor)—"Will you give me a glass of water?"
Barber—"What's wrong, sir? Hair in your mouth?"
Customer—"No. I want to see if my face leaks."

"Are you content to spend your life walking round the country begging?"

"Oh, no, lady. I'm saving up for a car!"

Boy Scout—"Pa, I shall have to lie down."
Pa—"Why, are you ill?"
Boy Scout—"No, but I've done so many good turns today that I feel giddy."

★ ★ ★

Bore—"I can do anything I set my mind on."
Listener—"Have you ever tried slamming a revolving door?"

★ ★ ★

Boss—"What do you mean by going out and getting your hair cut in the firm's time?"
Office Boy—"Well, it grows in the firm's time, doesn't it?"

"I always seem to strike the ball on top. How can I put that right?"

"You could try turning the ball upside down, mister."

Lady—"So you are the survivor of a shipwreck. Tell me, how did you come to be saved?"
Tramp—"I missed the boat!"

★ ★ ★

Motorist—"May I offer you a lift, sir?"
Absent-Minded Professor—"No, thank you. I have no use for one. I live in a bungalow."

★ ★ ★

"Are you the waiter who took my order?"
"Yes, sir!"
"H'm, still looking well, I see. Had a nice holiday?"

"You know, it says here that in London a man is knocked down by a car every five minutes."

"Gosh! He must be tough to stand up to that!"

1

2

3

4

Only one of these five shadows corresponds to the picture. Which one is it?

5

DOUBLE TROUBLE!

And these six pictures all look the same, but one is different. Can you find it?

A

F

B

C

D

E

ANSWERS — 3 AND E

Doctor, doctor, everyone thinks I'm a cricket ball.

How's that?

Oh, not you as well!

AHA! WULLIE! I'VE BEEN LOOKIN' FOR YOU!

AHEM—AT SIX-THIRTY ON THE EVENING OF THE TENTH, YOU WERE WITNESSED KICKIN' A CLOOTIE BA' IN THE DIRECTION OF......

WAIT! YE'RE WASTIN' YER TIME...

MY PUIR WEE LADDIE'S LOST HIS MEMORY...

WHO IS THIS TALL GENTLEMAN...?

JUST THEN—

HI, WULLIE....

ER—DO I KNOW YOU?

HE'S LOST HIS MEMORY, ECK!

JIST MY LUCK! THAT MEANS HE WINNA REMEMBER HE OWES ME FOWER JEELY BABIES!

WELL, I CANNA STAND HERE A' DAY —I'D BETTER GET READY!

RIGHT! I'M AWA'!

WOW!

WHIT'S GOIN'ON?

WAIT—YOU'LL SEE!

ZOOM

IT'S THE ROVER'S CUP-TIE TODAY —AND BANDY BAIRD, THEIR NEW FORWARD, IS PLAYIN'!

I THOUGHT THAT WID JOG YER MEMORY.

OH—ER— GULP!

HMM! THAT WIS A FAST RECOVERY!

YE'LL DAE DOUBLE FIDDLE PRACTICE A' WEEK—AND I WINNA FORGET THAT!

HO-HO! PA STILL TOOK ME TAE THE GEMME—AND WE HAMMERED THEM ONE-NIL!

CLACK! CLACK! CLACK!

What do you get if you dial 38956279146325089096304 7?

A sore finger!

OOR WULLIE'S CROSSWORD

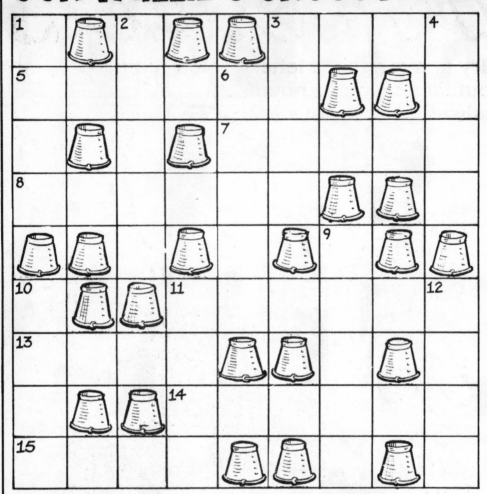

CLUES ACROSS

3. Finishes (4), 5. Land surrounded by water (6), 7. Eskimo house (5),
8. Come out (6), 11. Assault (6), 13. An object of admiration (4), 14. Your
T V needs one (6), 15. Scrambled or fried? (4).

CLUES DOWN

1. Measurement of distance (4), 2. Group of ships (5), 3. Rim (4), 4. Walk
wearily (4), 6. Opposite of day (5), 9. Fast (5), 10. Pleasant (4), 11. Sadly
(4), 12. Oven (4).

SOLUTIONS

ACROSS: 3. Ends, 5. Island, 7. Igloo, 8. Emerge, 11. Attack, 13. Idol.
14. Aerial, 15. Eggs. DOWN: 1, Mile, 2, Fleet, 3, Edge, 4, Slog, 6. Night.
9, Rapid, 10, Nice. 11, Alas, 12, Kiln.

TV TEASER

Try to arrange the letters below to find out the name of a popular television programme.

Answer: WHO WANTS TO BE A MILLIONAIRE?

Rhyme Time

OOR Wullie's been re-writing some well-known nursery rhymes, but he's left out some of the words. Can you fill in the blanks?

SING A SONG OF SIXPENCE, A POCKET
   FULL OF RYE,
FOUR AND TWENTY BLACKBIRDS, BAKED
   IN A PIE.
WHEN THE PIE WAS OPENED, THE KING HE
   LICKED HIS LIPS,
AND HOLLERED OUT, "YOU HAVE THE
   PIE,
AND I'LL HAVE B- - - - AND C- - - -."

HUMPTY DUMPTY SAT ON A WALL,
HUMPTY DUMPTY HAD A GREAT FALL.
ALL THE KING'S HORSES AND ALL THE KING'S BUNCH,
HAD A SMASHING O - - - - - - - FOR L - - - -.

LITTLE JACK HORNER SAT IN A CORNER,
EATING HIS CHRISTMAS PIE.
HE STUCK IN HIS THUMB
TO PULL OUT A PLUM,
AND THE JUICE SQUIRTED RIGHT IN HIS - - - -.

OLD MOTHER HUBBARD
WENT TO HER CUPBOARD
TO GET HER POOR DOGGIE A BONE.
BUT WHEN SHE GOT THERE,
THE CUPBOARD WAS BARE
SO SHE GAVE THE B - - - - - - A P - - - -.

Answers

1. beans and chips; 2. omelette for lunch; 3. eye; 4. butcher a phone.

PAPER CAPER!

HERE'S A FUNNY CAPER WITH PENCIL AND PAPER!

FIRST GET A PIECE OF THICK PAPER ABOUT 5″ X 3½″, THEN TRACE THE THREE FIGURES BELOW ON TO IT AS SHOWN, ONE ON THE FRONT AND TWO ON THE BACK. NOW CUT AND FOLD THE PAPER AS INDICATED. THE FUN STARTS WHEN YOU TURN THE FLAPS OVER—YOU'LL GET SOME REALLY ODD-LOOKING FOLK!

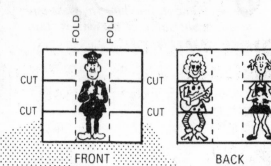

FOLD FOLD

CUT CUT

CUT CUT

FRONT   BACK

DOUBLE TROUBLE

ONLY TWO OF THE PICTURES OF WULLIE AND HIS PALS ARE EXACTLY ALIKE. CAN YOU SPOT THEM?

ANSWER: C AND H.

OOR WULLIE

The sun beats doon, it's affy hot,
But leave it tae oor chappie.
He knows how to cool right doon –
Just keep a big dog happy!

What do spacemen play in their spare time?

Astronaughts and crosses!

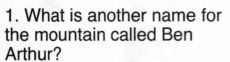

QUIZ BIZ!

Come on, all you brain-boxes, get your thinking caps on for Oor Wullie's special Scottish quiz. Nae peeking at the answers now!

1. What is another name for the mountain called Ben Arthur?
2. **Who wrote "Peter Pan"?**
3. What is the county town of Fife?
4. **Who invented the telephone?**
5. Which Scottish town was recently made a city?
6. **What is a "wag-at-the-wa"?**
7. What famous Shakespearean play is set in Scotland?
8. **Where does the Queen stay when she comes to Edinburgh?**
9. What famous Scotsman was a pioneer of television?
10. **What kind of flower is a "gowan"?**

11. What is a "puddock"?
12. **Which is the oldest university in Scotland?**
13. Which Scot gave his name to a type of rainwear?
14. **In which Scottish city is the Usher Hall?**
15. What is the national flag of Scotland?
16. **What was a leerie?**
17. Name the three "J's" for which Dundee is famous.
18. **What sport is played at Cathkin Park?**
19. Inch Cape, off the mouth of the River Tay, is better known as what?
20. **What were the McCrimmons of Skye famous for?**

QUIZ ANSWERS

1. The Cobbler. 2. J.M. Barrie. 3. Cupar. 4. Alexander Graham Bell. 5. Inverness. 6. A kind of pendulum wall clock. 7. "Macbeth". 8. Holyrood Palace. 9. John Logie Baird. 10. A daisy. 11. A frog. 12. St Andrews. 13. Charles Macintosh. 14. Edinburgh. 15. The Cross of St Andrew. 16. A man who lit the old gas street lamps. 17. Jam, jute and journalism. 18. Football. 19. Bell Rock. 20. Piping.

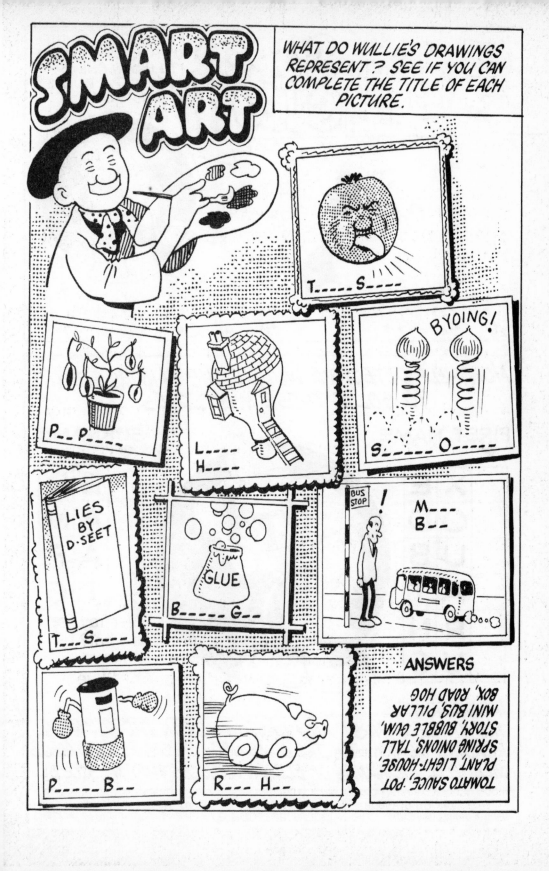

SNIFF! SNIFF!

SUPER SLEUTH

CONNECT ALL OF THE DOTS IN THEIR ORDER TO DRAW ONE OF DETECTIVE WULLIE'S ASSISTANTS.

NOW HELP DETECTIVE WULLIE, THE FAMOUS SLEUTH, TO SOLVE THESE MYSTERIES.

FIRST NAME. ▼

	X	E
	O	D
	U	B
	A	T
	R	N
	U	G

SURNAME. ▼

E	D
A	M
A	R
I	G
E	T

Answers below

IF YOU PRINT THE THIEF'S FIRST AND LAST NAMES IN THE SQUARES READING DOWNWARDS, THE COMBINED LETTERS READING ACROSS, WILL SPELL THE NAMES OF ELEVEN ARTICLES THAT HE STOLE.

First name: Stolen articles were; AXE, ROD, TUB, HAT, URN, RUG. Surname: Stolen articles were; BED, RAM, OAR, WIG, NET. Detective answer: ARTHUR BROWN.

OOR WULLIE

...e audience goggle when they see ...e strongman's demonstration. ...t when he tries one final feat — ...ings, there's consternation!

HMM. THERE'S AN IDEA! I'LL MAK' MY AIN MUSCLE- BUILDIN' DRINK AND SELL IT TAE THE LADS!

MAX'O' GIVES YOU MUSCLES
LOOK FOR THE BULGING BOTTLE

THERE'S NOTHIN' LIKE GUID, FRESH WATER!

WULLIE'S SHED

I'LL PIT ON A SHOW TAE DEMONSTRATE MY STRENGTH. BUT I'LL HAE TAE WEAKEN THIS PLANK FIRST...

MIGHTY MIX

...AND MAK' A TON WEIGHT OOT O' THIS CARDBOARD BOX.

2 DOZ PEACHES
1 TON
BLACK PAINT WHITE PAINT

TWA BALLOONS MAK' A FINE PAIR O' DUMB- BELLS!

GLUE
ASSORTED BALLOONS

HERE THEY COME!

A FREE SHOW BY THE MAKER OF MIGHTY MIX THE DRINK THAT GIVES YOU MUSCLES SPECIAL OPENING OFFER— TWO BOTTLES —6 PENCE

A FREE SHOW, EH! THIS HAD BETTER BE GUID!

AND NOW, LADEEZ AND GEN'LEMEN, WONDER WULLIE WILL DEMONSTRATE THE POWERS OF MIGHTY MIX...

AULD SHIRT WITH DABS OF BLACK PAINT

1 TON

GET ON WI' IT!

Why do spiders like the Internet?

They like visiting all the websites

Doctor, doctor, I've sprained my ankle. What should I do? Limp!